Within the Cave Something Pulses

Poems

Ryan Van Lenning

Copyright © 2025
by Wild Nature Heart Press

All rights reserved.
Use of this material with attribution is welcome.

For inquires, contact *ryan@wildnatureheart.com*

Cover Design by author

ISBN: 979-8-9934900-2-1

WildNatureHeart.com

Other Books By the Author

In the Re-Membering Series:
Re-Membering
One Bright and Real Caress
From Inside These Wild Ones

Other:
*Trust the Ceremony, F*ck the Ceremony, Trust the Ceremony*
An Ambitious Silence
Then Yeses Come Bubbling
Becoming Beautiful Barbarians (forthcoming)

In the Kin Collection:
Moon Has a Long Memory
Don't Forget the Smalls In Your Basket of Whos
Seasonocracy
Riverever
All the Stones in Us Are Birds
And Love Is a Tree Is a Human Is

*"The Long Dark is a place of waiting, silence, vigil, and alert witnessing.
Something is here, a vital and animating presence is here, in the dark-ness."*
~Francis Weller

CONTENTS

- INTRODUCTION 1
- THE PATH TO THE CAVE 2
  - What the Cave Evoked 3
  - A Single Leaf 5
  - The Soil of Us 6
  - Invoke All Your Inner Fungi 8
  - Carve Your Beautiful, Dark Cave 10
  - Forage the Listenings 12
  - Let the Season Season You 13
  - The Moon Has A Long Memory 15
  - You Wanted to See 17
  - October's Darkening Waters 19
  - Cold and Holy Unknowing 20
  - Threshold of a Season 22
  - Sacred Anchor 23
- THE BIG RHYTHM HOLDS IT ALL 27
  - I. Sip the Season Darkly 28
  - II. Within the Cave Something Pulses 30
- LABYRINTHOCENE 32
  - Sling Us Down, Gravity 33
  - Cartographic Promiscuities 35
  - Each Inch Its Own Center 37
  - A Thousand Glorious Threads 40
  - Self-Excavation 42
  - Labyrinth Politics 44
  - Regenerative Lostness 46

- Surrendering Strategies 49
- Tools and Pools..51
- Clue/Clew 53
- Her Sacred Labyrinth 56

PLAYGROUND OF BELOVED MONSTERS 58
- Playground of Beloved Monsters...................................59
- Whale of a Thing 60
- Truth Be Told 61
- Long-Lost Fingers of the Sun..62
- I Am Murder...63
- Of Mood and Molting Under Unborn Sky 65
- Some Big Heart Must Be Leaking................................66
- Three-Headed Hound 68
- Allowing Prophetic Artistry to Germinate From Our Magnificent Failures 70

DREAMFIRE 72
- Your Darkness Is Shining...73
- The Deeper We Crawl 75
- A Crack and Hidden Yes 76
- A Riff-Raff On Rifts and Rafts 77
- We Dream the Butterfly 79
- Dear Mud 81
- So, Crack 84
- Earth Will Soon Pour You Out 87
- The Path Is Made 88
- I Dispute This Passage No More 89
- Flashes Buried Here 91
- That Poem Under Your Skin 93

Serviceable Conduit 95
  The Gift 96
  The Experiment Isn't Over 98
  Rising Like a Blessing, Unbidden 99
About the Author 101
About Wild Nature Heart.. 102
Titles in the *Re-Membering* Series................................ 103
Excerpts From The Author's Other Books..................... 107

INTRODUCTION

Within the Cave Something Pulses is a seasonal spelunking of the darkness, a wandering in the labyrinth, and tender tending of the dreamfires that emerge in the fruitful darkness.

What if we allied ourselves to the energies of the season?

What if we dove into the silent dark and welcomed the wholeness of who we are?

What labyrinth wisdoms await?

What dreams are fires in the dark?

What if our shadow was an offering, and monsters were actually the secret password?

What emerges in the fruitful darkness?

The season is turning, both outside and within, and both personally and collectively. Autumn's march toward the deep dark womb of winter invites an Underworld transformation. A cave comes beckoning.

We embrace the dark to find renewal and our own sacred. We go to the cave for the descent into ourselves, to rest, to greet the wounds and monsters, but also uncover the shimmering treasures to bring back as gifts to the world as medicine.

THE PATH TO THE CAVE

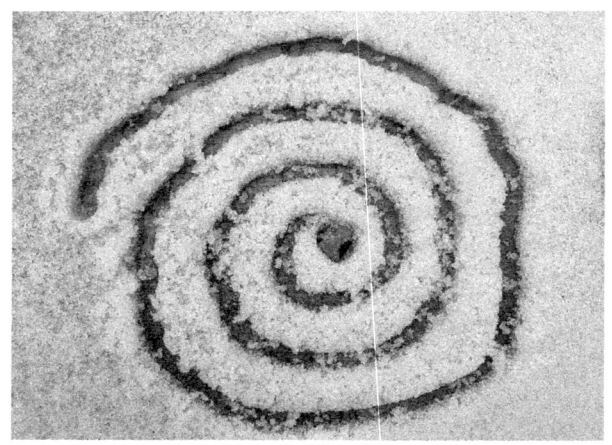

What the Cave Evoked

My name is Thrum and I am a claustrophiliac. I carry volcanoes in my heart, deep time in my blood. My great-great-great grandmother was a sacred spelunker. I am inside Earth.

Or is Earth inside me?

I recently explored caves and lava tubes in Lava Beds National Monument in NE California. Someone asked, what did the cave evoke?

First, other-than-sight senses begin to flash on, extending their feelers like tentacles of an undersea creature, while the eyes savor final details allowed by a fleeing light. As birdsong disappears above, one imagines hearing tides deep within.

Then that edge, alive and growing, creeps up the basement of the body.

Is it anxiety? Excitement? Vitality?

A part of me is consumed with fear. Wants to run out. It's real. It's information. My nervous system is on. But my nervous system isn't only mine. It is co-terminous with basalt and bats and hydrophobic bacteria.

I play with that edge, becoming curious with it.

Awareness of breath becomes acute. I swear I smell the scent of oxygen. The changing temperature indicates this is new territory. Frigid. This is not a land for humans.

Yet also, ancient memories of our human lineage running through caves—from protection to sur-thrival, from art to initiation. Indeed, who we are was born here.

Then arrives the awe of shape-shifting (trans)formations, the deep time invitations. I'm a split second in a symphony of creation.

To be in the bowels of an earth, vital and afire, despite the cold hard facts of being surrounded on all sides by seemingly immutable slick walls.

I experiment with the erotics/exotics of enclosure and what it means to be inside one another.

Finally, not least at all, an abiding, deep silence. It is here, in the darkest quiet, I sense, that all things are born.

I recall the Inuit and Inupiaq peoples of the far north have a custom in preparation for whale hunts. With no lamps lit, they sit in darkness, in stillness, in qarrtsiluni, the state waiting for something to happen. One translation of qarrtsiluni: "sitting together in darkness waiting for something to burst" until melodies and words rise like bubbles in the sea. Such are whales honored with song.

What else might honored with an audacious abiding in the dark?

Darkness is patient.

What is waiting to burst? What song is bubbling? What emerges in the fruitful darkness?

A Single Leaf

A single leaf
inaugurates the colossal powers of decay

falling right through the bottom
of summer, wide as life
deep as death

Sink your ear into its runaway veins—
that old hungry bell is booming
and pulling its great green garments up

Can you hear it echoing off the walls
of our luscious huts?

How it pulls the world
with unthwartable desire
into the momentous night?

How it circles the seasons around it
with well-shaped gravity?

It signals that great circle time
is on the hunt
in the shape of a cottonwood leaf

the color of life and death
singing its ephemeral and forever song

The Soil of Us

Do you think we're done breaking down
and building up?

A forest floor this rich
doesn't happen in a season
and we're still hungry for more—

that hard ground of wound
and wicked resistance
is many a meal to us

If grief and growth are sisters
inseparable
then we are their brother bond,
compost

It's ok, all of us are split.

All of us are half of a half,
and halves of those in turn

We're filled with detritus
all the way down like turtles—
it makes of us many a continent
and the water washing over

Darkness doubles, enfolding us
into its pocket
ever-deepening

Slip into it—Not with fear
nor like a thief

But like one resigned
to the Great Seasoner

Always breaking down
and building up

until the soil of us can grow
the whole truth

Keep breaking
again and again
until we hold it all.

Invoke All Your Inner Fungi

Recite the rotten motto
to earn the bright bloom

This era of decay,
this quiet and sometimes raucous
breaking down and going under

without which, no glorious spring
no unblemished blossom

certainly no sunworthy fruit
or feast will come

Recite the rotten motto
to earn the bright bloom

The dirty truth is
the soil of your next self
must be amended with death

No, you didn't ask for this
Grand Intimacy—the rules were here
when you arrived

So throw the year's dead and dying
on the heap
spelling compost in your blood
and invoke all your fungi

whispering the vows:

I will not turn up my nose
at worms

will not condescend to bacteria

will not avert my eyes
from the bloody beak in the remains

or the dazzling black beetles of me
in their delicious decomposition

I owe them all this poem,
my life

Carve Your Beautiful, Dark Cave

The path to the dark cave
starts innocently enough
with a sign full of useful information
in broad daylight, blue skies.

A fulfilling breakfast—
Small potatoes and duck eggs perhaps,
wild berries plump with promise.

Before you know it
you can hardly remember
the color of berries or eyes
or the sound of the river flowing.

Bats reign here
and the dominant thoughts
are of a bed and that last meal.

Feel the shape of those walls
textured by the smooth slink of years
moist with mysterious things
you'd rather not know.

To either side, tunnels to treasures
or traps.

There's no way to know
and no sure way out
other than following the scent
of the deepest voice with you.

The deeper you spelunk
the brighter the darkness.

Hard pains, sweet pains
nectars maybe, but first the cuts
both slow and quick deaths.

Sometimes monsters
and the secret password
are the same thing.

Of course, you could avoid the path altogether
by staying "at home"

But don't think darkness is avoidable.

Or are you one who believes in light
without the dark?

Trailheads without wounded trailfeet,
mountain views without valleys?

Oh, what an imagination!

Come now!

Carve your beautiful, dark cave
and then come home, my friend
with well-earned feet
and a heart that knows.

Forage the Listenings

The hour arrives to turn the volume down
in order to hear.

The season of silence begins
with a low guttural
and the treetops glistening—
you go in foraging the listenings.

Some silver-bladed violence begins evaporating
the tangled knots unravel.

Now in the dark,
you see your bright thread
weaving the important things.

Things un-split
and a mammal presence fills your cave.

Like a long-forgotten season,
a deep rest emerges.

When that hour arrives
the bones signal their agreement,
melodies erupt from within
and all your ears open.

You enter foraging the listenings.

Let the Season Season You

Don't jump over the season
like an escapee.

You may dream of spring
on the solstice

try for eternal vernal
at the first frost
but you can't leap beyond the now.

Slow down
and let the season season you.

There is much that is not true
until darkness gets its due

yet, there is hope in truth
and dark's your better ally
than unseasonal false friends.

So don't jump over the season
like an escapee.

From what are you fleeing?

Can you flee from the season within you?

Don't be tempted by the empty calories
of bittersweet fruit too easily procured—
an early ripening causing indigestion.

Let the season season you.

Let the cold crack that hard bark
of yours—open your meadow
to feel it all.

Open your earthbody and feel
even the best of it
as well as the worst of it—
where it hurts the most.

Oh how much life there is
in death!

Be still and let the season season you.

Let darkness fall in you
like a sword of truth
and you will find a deeper root
than you ever knew.

Then—at the ripening hour
your branches will know
how to celebrate the sky

your sun will be a true sun
the world is needing most.

Do you understand
these are the kindest words
you've yet heard?

The Moon Has A Long Memory

The moon has a long memory
and hasn't forgotten your true name

It is mere habit to shrink when the sun sinks

Have you tried standing up
and meeting the gaze of the Swordsman
when he asks you:

what luster's tucked under
your supernova skin?

Have you considered lifting the lid
off your day-time self
stitched tight oh too tight and oh—

Or are you only a lover of butterflies
despiser of bats?

One of the half-time lovers of the world?

Then by all means, bless your mangled life
half-bitten and hungry

If not, pour pitch black down
your poor back
and feel your ancient arch grow

The moon has a long memory
and hasn't forgotten your name—

the one you uttered so assuredly
back in the season of jumping

before the great gremlins of approval
stole it from you with foggy breath

Be big with midnight
and tempt the stars out with Cheshire desire

Behold, some belly bold
cries your full name from the old
deeplier than ever told—

Perhaps it is your own

You Wanted to See

You stayed late.

Yes, you wanted to see.

To see what would happen
once your sun went down.

The same thing always happens
when you wait too long to leave—

things disappear

silhouettes emerge

a cunning darkness delivers up slices
of woolly silent parts
that now have something to talk to

or at least echo achingly
inside their own crooked canyons

as you trip over roots
because your feet forgot their eyes.

Eventually it comes up again.

The light. The hope.

Yet you wonder if a conversation ever happened.

Memories are paper cuts.

Memories are hugs.

Eventually it comes up again—
but never exactly where you think

never shining on the same you
that is never exactly what you think either.

You wanted to see.

October's Darkening Waters

Afloat on October's darkening waters
where no preludes live, only conclusions

It's a wonder how often one forgets
that sometimes just to endure
is a full-time gig

when the wood mouse once again escapes
the talons from the sky

when air is served grey and husky
and whatever dreams were sent downstream
towards the sea in seasons past

return as trickster scenes from film noir
relentless and edged
with an burnt amber dark humor

and what might possibly be red and green
in the disturbed wild

can barely be made out
through mind-thick fog
in which only ravens speak.

Cold and Holy Unknowing

Sometimes when light takes a turn
you want it even brighter

But when dark wraps itself
around you like a cocoon

you want it deeper
than the Mariana Trench

For to hear any true thing
requires a rare and robust silence

one that flees
from sun's boisterous embrace

In the temple of darkness
your stone vessel cracks

as some heartbody grows round
and smooth with sacred slugs, whispers

The hibernaculum is the school
of the unseen and undone

without which nothing
is really seen or done

For light is far too loud
for a bear on the perimeter to bare

and even deepest of autumn eyes
see all-too-boldly

when things are settling in
for the cold and holy unknowing

Threshold of a Season

So you've come to the threshold of a season

Take a cue from Sister Aspen
and lay all your old answers down

You've received an invitation from darkness
to winter well—the cave comes calling

Enter the cave with a child's heart
and a warrior's wound

Asking all the impossible questions
impervious to troublesome answers

Fatten yourself up with them
and curl up for a mountain's rest

You will find that winter was waiting for you as well
and needs your warmth

The fire around which the season turns
dances in your belly

The company you keep
will become the soil of spring

The dreams you cook together
will become the tulip's tip

For now, it is enough to know
that the cave is equally your home
within which so much lives

Sacred Anchor

I. Ripe For Descent

All the world long has descent on its mind

and you with it:

the freckled hands of deep autumn
the fickle lure of an underground love
pull you down
with the Western star.

Who are you to argue
when the trajectory has gravity on its side?

II. Without the Journeyed Dark

There never was a sunrise
without the journeyed dark.

There never was a spring
without the starried night.

There never was a buried treasure
without the sunken ship.

There never was a deepest love
without the sink or swim.

III. Pace of the World

You are of a pace with the world now.

Who are you not to follow Sun,
or the season's decadent fragrance
into the dark?

It's a different kind of allure
at the bottom of things
inside out and beautiful.

Decay is a gift from the soul
of the world

You find yourself
making the vow: you will not be caught
being a full-time harvester,
no ever-ascender.

The soil needs rest
like the dark halls of your heart,
washed with riotous rains.

IV. Her Depths Now

These are her depths now!

There was a time when light
—any light—
was a buoy, a wondrous distraction.

Now: a thieving beast
robbing you of Elder Darkness.

These are her depths now,
you bark at the sun.

Have you no thought to buried treasures?

Are you one of the light-brigade,
ever casting gold through your fingers?

Today, with the wind's decree
and consent of the moon
you hook yourself willingly, even eagerly
to the Sacred Anchor.

To the Sun-Addicts, you say:

I now follow Moon,
stalking the territory of forbidden night-songs

meeting all the beasts born
of the soil.

IV. Dark Mirrors

Yes, the bottom of the season is cruel.

But it is not the first labyrinth, nor the last.

Some song echoes a refrain: "I know my powers"
from the caverns below.

Just the right amount of forgetfulness
and remembering fills the chambers.

Then, from the coldest corner,
the darkest thing whispers to you.

V: The End of the Descent

The end of the descent is self-embrace.

The bottom of the well
is the face of love
looking back.

It catapults you to the inside
of a cherry blossom
just this side of spring.

THE BIG RHYTHM HOLDS IT ALL

A Solstice Ceremony

I. Sip the Season Darkly

Darkness has arrived
wrapping its inky cloak
across the season of our lives

long shadows and owls
stand tall and salute
the arc of autumn's slow song
becoming winter's long march

asking us not skip too quickly over the hour

with an eager eye grasping
towards plum blossoms awaiting on the other side

Drink deeply from the season,
they say

Drink from the cup overflowing
with the sweet and fruitful darkness

Sip the season darkly
in its slow embrace

Wisdom hidden from summer's glare
may yet pass our lips
should we have the thirst for it

The bright and busy world goes under:

We go to the cave, the secret one
in the mountain of ourselves
seeking stillness

and listen for it—
the true voices amidst

The Silence.

Can you hear them?

II. Within the Cave Something Pulses

We've been here before.

Many times—as far back
as it will be forever forth.

The Big Rhythm holds it all.

Within the cave something pulses.

We hear it, feel it, even now

that which deepest dark cannot smother
and even winter's hands cannot touch

tender tendrils of a luscious vine
bearing the wine of our heart

Some secret vial distilled for this very hour
to sip the season brightly

A Remembering—Aha!

Sun too misses its lover earth
and cannot too long stay away.

Like you, Sun was meant for this: to shine.

To not share that big love is a wounding.

So in this darkest hour
Sun knocks on the nearest horizon
announcing The Return with a steady beat:

"Dear Love, I'm Here."

Which is exactly what we find
written on the walls of our cave:

"Dear Love, I'm Here"

As we open new eyes
like the first breath after coma

and though it's just a whisper now
it is enough to start it all again
and again…again….again…

LABYRINTHOCENE

Labyrinthocene explores our personal and collective initiation through the image of the Labyrinth and through mythopoetic and liberatory lenses. Variously called the Great Unraveling or the Long Dark, the moment we are in invites a regenerative lostness and falling off of inherited maps—these explorations are hands to the slick walls of the cave, kiss to the snout of the monster, asking what threads might be available for a return.

Sling Us Down, Gravity

As meaning-makers, knowing what story we're in matters. Seeking the evermore, the god, the treasure at the center of the labyrinth are popular tales. Heroes and ascent, slay the dragon, become the king, etcetera.

Yet, 'up' is almost as boring as 'straight'; and even the end of the world has happened so many times.

Because we are master denies (homo denialicus), to ask that we live summer yearlong, to go forever flying without touching mud and monsters is also wishful thinking.

Imagine if we withdrew our consent to this ubiquitous denialism?

Imagine all this monumental energy we give to not looking. Not feeling. How might it be marshalled in liberatory ways?

What if we kissed monsters on the snout and withheld our participation in the league of forgetting, beginning a grand Era of Repair?

After all, sometimes monsters and the secret password are the same thing.

Sometimes mud or a virus slows us down long enough to not rush into cages of engrained and inherited nervous system habits, enacting incarcerations and so many species of fight and flight.

The promise of mud and monsters is an authentically crooked caress of the wound and a profound and earthy intimacy.

So yes, sling us down, gravity, we no longer resist the labyrinthine turns and ups and downs.

We can witness. We can pay attention. We can play attention. We can experiment with Life.

We will tell each other: If you're going north, trust your north. If you're going south, trust your south. If you're going west, trust your west. If you're going east, trust your east.

We will say: you're safe and unsacrificeable.

The tug, the tongue of the beast, the troubling truth—we trust because we are already home.

Let us vow chants of holy demolition. Let us vow unreasonable embrace.

Let us vow becoming generously and regeneratively lost.

Let us fling gratuitous gossamer threads of remembering throughout this dark labyrinth.

Opening to the magnetic pull, let us know once again what sacred footsteps feel like.

Cartographic Promiscuities

It's understandable—no one really wants to be lost in the labyrinth. For thrill seekers it might be exhilarating, but for most of us disorientation and free fall is terrifying—best saved for the roller coaster and the sky dive. Or the love affair.

A luscious surrender is required.

Despite being abundantly adorned with daffodils and road signs, the darkness here is deep. Yet Deep Lost is the pre-condition of deep belonging, if only we'd admit it. If only we'd open the invitation disguised as devastation.

The invitation reads: You are catastrophically invited to Fall through the map into new territories. It is addressed to all of us. But it gives no address.

When we're not ready to enter the abyss of the not-yet-known, we commit to a zealous anchoring into the known—monogamous with known coordinates as a safety measure. Even if we're bored, even if we're suicidal, at least it's familiar.

But this house of modernity wasn't meant to be an eternal marriage, but an experimental affair. This Highway of Death isn't the only way to travel the world.

There were signs at the beginning, easy to miss as we sped by. One said: "It may never be enough."

Another: "You may lose everything by taking everything."

We ignored them. But now there's a knowing effervescing in us; a knowing that we've exhausted the parameters of that map. A remembering unfurling its tendrils towards the sun of erotic landscapes of liberation.

Our polypoetic pollinating urges toward life and liberation are getting out of hand.

Out of map. Out of prison.

By honoring those sensual strange beasts we are offering the world something so gratuitously beautiful, so utterly breath-giving and stunning the seventh generation is sitting around the fire singing songs about it.

It's not just that we have to look for new signs pointing to off-ramps. We can become cartographically promiscuous, conjuring new signs, flinging latitudes of love and longitudes of liberation like reckless fern spores, geotagging coordinates that aren't yet subsidized by the ink of habit, practicing connecting right-here-right-there with filaments of glistening audacity that serve as pathways towards…

Each Inch Its Own Center

First thing folks wanna do is turn on the lights.
Even though that's how the stars died.

That's called outsourcing your wisdom
and we need your wisdom.

We say eat. Eat the darkness like a worm
working its way through an apple.

Kick up that appetite. Fill up
with the cool calories of its dense flesh.

This is no time for light
diets—become fat

with dark's delicious silence.
You're gonna need the strength

for the return journey.
For now, when you least expect it

you'll drop into a cavity
landing in the core

You'll know it's a center
because the sound of trust

echoes off the walls
suddenly your eyes blink open

and you can stand
in the blunt and bright truth of things

nowhere can fear be found
and a certain familiar struggle disappears.

A treasure awaits but it's not
what you thought

Like the worm encountering the seed
too large to eat, too heavy to carry.

It is not yours to take,
and you find yourself cherishing it,

but wanting it for others.
You take one last look around

and take the first sure step
since the clock struck midnight

with the true treasure,
not the one you have

but the one you have become
for having taken the journey.

For having followed your longing.
For having trusted your feet

that conjured the path
that lead you here.

For turning poison that fueled your getaways
into potions that fuel your giveaways.

Knowing that even now,
just as you have found your bearings

a new journey begins.
But now you know

what trust tastes like
on the tongue

How to die and give up
on knowing

Know how to crawl inchédly
along the edges of each turn

caressing the slick walls in the dark
each inch etching something holy.

Each step its own center.

A Thousand Glorious Threads

It's dark in here.
That much we can agree on.

It's easy to want to panic.

To grasp about for threads
hitting your head hard on things
a step in any direction.

But please please
don't follow the wrong thread home.

It's so easy to miss your thread
when you are seeking anything
not to feel this way.

Humbling to learn yet again
that forgetting is as relentless as winter.
Yet remembering is as persistent as spring.

Feel your beautiful arch grow.

You were meant for this.

You are already at the opening
because you already are at the heart.

The thread is not a trend or trope.
The thread is not someone else's hope.

It cannot be consumed, only created—
spun from your abdomen.

(Where the silk comes from is a mystery)

It is not a person or a plan.

Give up on superheroes,
purge all perfect things.

A thousand glorious threads
but they are not all yours.

The thread is who you are.
What will kill you not to do.

Not to be.

Your way of going deeper into the world
is the thread that leads us out

like the light that trees keep deep
in their roots

calling us back home.

Self-Excavation

The art of going deep requires risk. Chthonic creatures demand sacrifice. Perhaps your ego; perhaps your plans. Perhaps the entire in-credible infrastructure of your identity.

Likely the maps you obtained along the way won't be of much use. You won't get it right. And it won't be pretty. But you might become truly alive and aimed, should you have a big enough appetite for shadows and bone fragments and all the clawed, crawling things inside.

Sometimes getting stuck is a blessing. But then again, Curses and Blessings are not the distinct species crypto-biologists once believed.

Like hope/despair, mind/matter, order/disorder, subject/object, sacred/profane, victory/defeat, me/you, alive/dead—binaries hide whole worlds behind their skirts.

Worlds desperately seeking us.

But this descent, this rough initiation, this Chthulucene proliferates paradoxes. Was there ever an Elder, a Wizard or Witch who didn't know how to hold them? And since we've long buried them, it's up to us to become them.

Nothing is what it seems in the Underworld. Once it goes black, your eyes are of no use. Better to enlist your ears and gut; your sense of smell and humor; activate your mad dream skillz and slither sideways imprinting your belly in the sand.

Being ensnared can be a call to pay attention: what am I not noticing here? Where are my limbs? Who's here? Where has my heart fallen asleep?

Perhaps being meandered and mired IS the way. Floundering is being found, Lostness is luck.

Who knows, maybe Limit is a Lotus Flower.

Be prepared to slow dance with a shovel, a choreography of shifting sands and a jig of sweat and blood. You might need to eat bugs and rocks for a fortnight.

Dig! Dig! Dig! the chorus chants.

Surrender your aggressive micropolitics of self and let the cavernous wind knock you down.

If you discover a buried treasure, it's only so you can give it away. You don't own anything. And here all along you thought ownership was a real thing.

If you do make it out the other side (and we need you to), if the sun rises, it won't be without listening to the strange things howling in the night—and sometimes it's you.

Labyrinth Politics

Labyrinth politics is a species of radical democracy.

If we truly got that in our gut cells, by golly gee hi hither, we'd be standing in the bright darkness together, hips open and hearts akimbo.

As a friend put it recently eloquently: zero people know WTF.

Which levels the playing field quite a bit. As in: starting in a field of ignorance is the prerequisite for play. And play is condition for something new to emerge.

Just ask a child.

Or a god.

That god itself is 'figuring it out' with each step is something neither taught nor entertained. Yet what better entertainment than god becoming world becoming god? In this labyrinth, there is nothing to figure out. Only each step etching something holy.

Be careful what truths we let in, it might re-arrange our molecules. We are not yet practiced in so-called human democracy, let alone listening to our cosmic constituency.

Every voice counts, including those without vocal chords. Including nematodes and narcotics. Including high-tide black lichen and low-tide whales, stomach swollen with plastic. Including unexpressed rage and erotic longings, stars and SARS-CoV-2.

If that weren't enough, it gets more gelatinous—Every individual counts, including those who aren't individuals. Which is everyone. Or should we say, everythree.

In the politics of pronouns, 'we' is still under-represented in the confederacy of creation, yet to be reclaimed from royalty by the huddled masses.

We have never been individuals.

Just ask mom. Or your mitochondria.

We shall throw our confusions into the circle. Toss our concussions (Latin, 'a shaking, an earthquake') and intifadas (Arabic, also, a 'shaking off') into the cauldron, let it bubble.

We shall vote with the only currency we truly have—our presence.

We shall hold Council of the Blind leading the all-too-sighted.

We shall go through the motions of tallying the votes. Knowing it's just another word for Life in its ongoing emergence, without the terrible thwarting by lies of separation.

Regenerative Lostness

To say, "I am lost" is not something you're allowed to say in the OverCulture.

Certainly not "we are lost."

After all, the doctrine of discovery is embedded in its DNA, so 'finding' and 'knowing' are core values.

If you are lost that's one thing—entirely your fault—but leave us out of it.

So the story goes.

But when you're in the labyrinth, being with the darkness and practicing a sweet not-knowing is a prerequisite to the journey. Before the next footstep, utter, "I am lost."

As a whisper if we must; as a roar if we find the brutal truth of it in our belly.

This is not perfunctory; this is ecospiritual patterning.

Ecospiritual because both the stillness and subsequent steps are utterly subsidized by everything not human; patterning because the universe knows how to do that whole life/death/contraction/expansion/light/dark thing.

It's a species of surrender, also forbidden by the laws of empire.

The feeling of abject terror of doing so is understandable, as lostness is a species of death.

And we don't do death.

It's why we're in the labyrinth in the first place.

The panic and turning on all the halogens is also understandable, having hitched ourselves to shallow coordinates. Even if they have ruptured us from reality, they have helped us feel...what?

Safe? Powerful?

Could it be that the threat of being swallowed by all that uncertainty promises holds treasures beyond the anxieties of the current trajectory?

There is only one way to find out: practicing the devastation of not knowing.

This is a portal into a variety of spiritual event for which the Overculture has no word for and in fact relentlessly conspires against with substitutes and distractions.

Why? Because within it live the seeds of its own demise.

By some trickster grace a strangeness may unfold, some coalescence of mystery coaxed by our finally refusing to be in charge—the emergence of possibility.

Something new being encountered.

It might even be things we know beyond the knowing of it.

This is the bio-politics of regenerative lostness. From it issues that next right move.

A step. A stumble. A shedding.
A thread. A light. A new color.

Weaving us back into the bright and awe-full symphony of things.

Surrendering Strategies

It's an odd thing to say: give up on strategy. As realization of the labyrinth takes root (consciously, that is. Our bodies/psyches already know), talk like this seems the worst.

Given the (lack of) culture that shaped our psycho-physiology, it may be impossible even to hear it. But at this point in the labyrinth, allowing cultural forms to emerge that support collapse is just good manners.

We can't give up...anything. That requires accepting Limit, which is exactly what the Era of Light Modernity cannot do. The lack of limit is what built it all. Nonetheless, exactly what modernity can't do is the invitation.

Hmm...so where does that leave us?

That we're not in control and we can't do anything alone is something to notice; the sooner we find our way into surrender the better. Surrender all psycholinguistic strategies deployed to prop us up in the hierarchy of right and good.

We might sit at the altar of maple leaf and learn how to die properly.

That's the crux of this paradox, isn't it? Because we are creatures of Empire, we simply don't know how to genuinely and regeneratively genuflect.

That's where kinship with Other-wise powers comes in.

Of course, it's already here, making everything chug along, invoking, inviting, digesting, creating, destroying, entangling. But there's gonna be a lot less dirty pain if we notice this a little more politely.

Because everything desires to be seen (not visually), it wouldn't hurt to say hi and let them know we're open to play and being conquered.

This is about bowing to Water and our forehead kissing King Dirt. It's about becoming an obsessionate one, a fool for life.

It's about being slayed by Beauty, becoming permeable to impossibilities (awe-struck).

It's about being knocked over by wind, eaten by leviathans of grief, daring to hear songs of the legions of dead who refuse to remain buried.

It's about being sliced open and put back together by galactic creatures and micro-beasts and being undone by landscapes of erotic intelligence, swallowed by sunsets of ecosensual extravagance, and submitting to Dom Cosmos, tied up and ravaged speechless in frenzies of unfathomable mystery.

What kind of strategy is that?

It's not.

Tools and Pools

What's the most important tool for survival? It's a bit of trick question one asks when preparing folks for the wilderness. The answer: your mind.

If you get lost in the wild or something goes wrong it can very easy to panic—heart rate goes up, breathing accelerates, one begins to act quickly. Some will begin making poor decisions in that state of mind, charging irrationally with a body full of adrenaline in any direction, rather than slowing down, finding navigational markers, taking in the evidence, strategically charting a plan.

One aspect of that advice certainly transfers to labyrinth-wandering: slowing down. Without it, it's almost guaranteed we will replicate old paradigms and reinforce automatic and harmful habits.

But Underworld strategy is a whole different cup of nettle tea. First of all, to get out we have to go deeper. The center still awaits and hate to say it, but we ain't near there yet. So for the moment, forget about getting out.

Second, since it's pitch dark here, locating navigational markers aren't going to do us much good, as most visible beacons are stale signals leading us in circles, reinforcing walls. So we're going to have to relinquish our addiction to sight, and lean into hearing, touch, smell, intuition, proprioception, bat wisdom, and whale ears.

Third, since we're carrying around these deep pools of wisdom called bodies and hearts, we might as well get wet with their wisdom. Dip our feet in, tingling with sensation, then our head, picking up on subtle—then booming—signals from forgotten and extra-vagrant deep water soundprints.

We light our torches with dreams, arm ourselves with courage known only to the great lovers and dive in soul first.

Things lurk we can hardly fathom—terrible things that want to have a conversation with us and splendors that invite our positive regard in order to shapeshift into forms they feel comfortable letting sunlight touch.

We might take a lesson from Dolphins, who use head fat to regulate biosonar listening. Growing sea lungs, we dive down league by league, settling into the soul-tide depths of true voice.

Now that's a totally different answer to the trick question.

Clue/Clew

This poem is neither efficient nor convenient
and won't make things easier for us

It's doubtful it will get anything done
and it's not going to fit into a Saturday night gown

of 144 characters
or inspire us in half a second

it takes to scroll past its first line
against a Lo-Fi filtered sky

The end is built into it—like everything—
but so is the beginning

but we'll have to follow the thread
to get there

like Theseus
who we can be forgiven for not knowing

because he hasn't yet been played
by a well-muscled Brit in the theaters

but whom we might resemble
being so lost in a labyrinth we haven't yet noticed

so we're not yet truly looking
for a way out

but a tender pulse is looking
disguised inside our fourth stomach.

There may be a moment
when time slows down just enough

to allow the incessant filling in
to take a sacred pause

and the chasm seems a giant darkness
windowing into our turquoised truth

that we mistake as holy terror
instead of our holy caduceus.

We could try to google the meaning
or we could stay to play and wrestle.

Maybe the poem you are in
is itself the *clew providing clues one might follow

to escape the cavern
we didn't know we were in:

Like one thread suggesting
there is no escaping, only a shapeshifting

but not without first
looking the beast in the eye.

The sunset here is made up
of a hundred wide-winged birds

flying down the horizon
of our heart

soaring slyly into that sacred space
between the things we know all too well

and those other things
we don't want to know

slipping between them undetected
and unanticipated

Let's pick a bird or two and trust
their wingéd wisdom

clipping the stony walls
and feeling the cave expand

Let's join the cacophonous chorus
singing the sun up.

That it was plucked
from the head of the monster

in a daily ritual of beaks and blood
surprises us

That we are the bird
the cave
the monster
and the sun

surprises us even more.

*clew = ball of thread. This old English word shares a
root with Sanskrit, glauḥ, meaning lump.

Her Sacred Labyrinth

…And then I began walking ceremoniously towards her…

That which I feared, yet wanted
rested silently at the center

past the guardsmen and the hounds
with their illusory barks

I was already there
when the golden maple leaves
adorned her stunning shoulders
green with promise

The exact moment
we were born in each other
no one knows

but it carries the scent of cedar-mud
and the texture of manzanita skin

I had heard her beats
well-murmured from afar
like dreams caressing upon a shore

When a well-placed star
in the north coast fog
bled into me

signaling the first footsteps
into her sacred labyrinth

I learned how to step along

her riverine curves
and mountain-born mystery

carrying trust in open hands
like a deep autumn release
surrendering to a greater force

My feet following a heart
well-worn with the seasons

PLAYGROUND OF BELOVED MONSTERS

Playground of Beloved Monsters

What if we were to take our elegant demons out for a walk in the winter sun?

Practice playing footsie with all the beautiful ghouls that haunt our halls?

This is where we risk the syrupy ache of opening ever-more fantastic cracks out of which our most fearless frogs and moon-faced monsters crawl with whom we eventually fall in love.

This is where we discover that sometimes monsters and the secret password are the same thing.

The teeth of your favorite monsters at your neck?

Give them a breath mint and invite them to tea or mulled wine.

If you set the mood right, you might end up caressing each other's voluptuous sacred wounds.

Part Shadow Council, part Inner Bestiary, part Animist Apprenticeship, this is where we ask taboo questions:

What if we kissed our monsters on the snout?

What if we take them on a picnic and feed them wild shadowberries?

What if we welcomed our inner beasts home, re-enlisting them with our consciously-aligned values and vision?

Whale of a Thing

But gusts by belly blew him back
swallowed silver dull and dull
without mercy without slack
took him in, a whalefull

inside dimmed forgot the way
which the up and which the east
towards what amorphous scummy stuff
he knew not what, some grief at least

but what it lonelied or what it meant
was quite enough. So quite enough.

grey makes one wan and spent, to stick
to any darkly thing or form
or flee to any colored storm

but what resolve to only float
and let the whale swim and soar
to look in wide and wormly eyes
until spit back upon the shore

Truth Be Told

But truth be told I am plastic, I am supremacy,
i am a prison, i am a conspiracy,
i gorge when I could nibble,
i dodge and deny, gulp and grasp,
just to avoid the manic monsters that i never learned
are ambassadors from an ancient home,
little ones asking for guidance from the elders,
elders asking for an ear.
I am avoidance, i am cruelty,
I've stolen paradises from more chests
than I'll ever know
just to be one who knows.
i lie to be good to be loved to be okay, okay:
i am a weapon, i am a faithful forgetting,
i am a terrible myth unfolding,
i am an unlikely remembrance,
i am dream to include it all
and truth be told, i trust the dreamer.

Long-Lost Fingers of the Sun

So you wanna know
how these things happen—
All the Whys and What-fors?

When even now Raven rips up
a plastic tie inside my rusted chest,
left in the rain for weeks

or how the cracked wind
and long-lost fingers of the sun
compete for the attention of my skin, thin
as thick as ego

Or some word that describes
a part of the bark of me that says
I'm guilty, it's true

And I don't pretend to hide it
any more, any more than
the wind can cloak its scents,
Raven his croaked curiosity

But guilt isn't what it used to be
and the bright green how of it
hides behind his eyes—
if it exists at all.

I Am Murder

We're at the front of the funeral
standing in the tragedy but it wasn't you
and it wasn't them
it was I who pulled the trigger
I who killed you
I who killed them all off
I who conjured walls and razor wire
First across the landscape of my heart
and then across the landscape of our mother
it was I who didn't know what I was doing
all I know is we are bleeding out
and I hated everything they stand for
everything you are is what is wrong with this world,
I had said
I believed many things back then
yesterday was a long time ago
I didn't know how to metabolize the darkness yet
and I tell you this not as a confession
not as a cautionary tale
but because someone said the truth shall set us free
and maybe truth shall let me be
more deeply who i am
more honestly who we are
the truth makes all beings at peace
but regardless I have come to hate the lie
knowing I have lived so many lies
but the lie that I am letting die
is the one that puts concrete between you and me
because it's heavy and it hurts
and I'm not saying don't have anything between us
but if we have to put something there let it be rich soil
in which things might grow between us

and I don't care whether that's weeds or a sunflower
or mycelium or fucking hookworms
I'm just saying concrete and steel is cold and careless
I'm just saying I have killed enough
and I'm done murdering
I want to try something resembling love
I want to try being here on/with/as earth
Together

Of Mood and Molting Under Unborn Sky

Under this unborn sky
rainless rusted
without benefit of peach
or persimmon stains—
an anonymous creature remains
of mood and molting

The night stacks itself thick
with jugular memories
born husky and hooked to root
rough-hewn and lunatic

The creature lopes revoltingly towards
what appears to be a tool of war—
perhaps it's the moon, perhaps a dull rage or lust—
at the edge of the shadowed field
wielding it at first like an axe
then like a song
soon hooked to remembrance
itself hitched to hue and heft

Clouds gather robust and looming
heavy with dust and promise, proving
once and for all—
once they're moving
even silhouettes can spawn revolutions
wet with purpose

Some Big Heart Must Be Leaking

Walking through the rooms of night
you arrive at a dawn clipped
by forgetfulness

With pockets full of slivered moons
and winter shred

You notice empty hands and bare feet
nimble but numb
and without purpose

Yet tracks in the snow
mark a path from somewhere

And though it feels cold
a trickle of blood melts
into the stark white
convinced it is life—

Some big heart must be leaking.

Even the premise of yesterday's grand feast
has been forgotten
and tomorrow is so far away

You cannot even feign to paint hope
on your weary eyelids
scarred from memory's frost

Why can't you find today?
Did they forget to put it out?

Have you joined the ranks

of the zombie parade

or succumbed, finally
not to some bold virus
but to the unutterable utter mundane?

Not having a mirror
you cannot see
what this has done
to your ordinary beautiful face

but were you to guess the shape
of your eyes
the left would be nowhere to be found
and the right would be an empty cup

Have you misplaced them
or did some sly storm steal them away?

No matter, the hour has arrived
to empty your pockets
and go find and tend to
that wounded heart

Three-Headed Hound

That three-headed hound at the gate?

I know him well
as he is my own monster

The shape of his canine fangs fit
my perfect wounds

his faces of self-doubt, shame, and abandonment
gazes inward as much as out

But I am entering a larger world
so I invite him to dinner

And make a meal of him
swallowing his serpent tail as dessert

After wrestling for three long lifetimes
the deed is done

My swords are not unsharp
yet I used not iron
but a much more deadly weapon—
a hungry heart

Now, he is my loyal soldier
re-commissioned into the advanced guard
for the journey ahead

But I need not swagger
nor be overly bold

I know bigger shades await

that will not be so deterred

And the biggest—
that dark one at the bottom—
remains noisy

and so far, unloveable

Allowing Prophetic Artistry to Germinate From Our Magnificent Failures

"To be a utopian thinker is to be one interested in the study of failure. The poet often has to say to the historian: There were friendships at that site of failure, at the rebellion that didn't succeed. If you look at the clusters, there was poetry you missed, music you can't seem to hear. Starlight often isn't a part of the historical record." —Tikkun Bambara

This is the practice: allow prophetic artistry to germinate from our magnificent failures, to become sacred sprouts cracking through the paved road to new paradigms.

To become fungi flinging itself up through the forest floor of failure, flourishing as creative clusters in sites of collapse. To bow gently at sites of modest mistakes and to fall on dirty knees prostrating at sites of fantastic flops.

Like fruiting bodies of underground networks, our resurrections are rebellions of surprise and disguise and the prize it implies, creating pathways beyond the sight of authority.

In the record of our big fuck up, we excavate the poetry and music we may have missed while we were deep in it. The documentarians of defeat living within us often overlook the archives of beauty that allowed the magnificent mistake to even occur.

We study failure as the soil of grand gardens of higher education. Not as a to-do list or some smart strategy, but as a way of walking in the world as regular and revolutionary cute and pathetic beings.

As a way of waking up in a culture that would rather keep us numb and in a dull trance.

We're full of shit and full of galactic glitter, vast and beautiful openings in the cosmos, wondrous waves of awakening.

We're unnamed colors surthriving the grey, arrows aimed, wishing scars, spirals apprenticing to our stardust heartbeat, a free library of unbridled succulence.

We let the buzzing bees of us transmute the nectar of cunning catastrophe into the honey of our next deepest path.

With the new goal: To fail big-time on a game few are yet playing.

DREAMFIRE

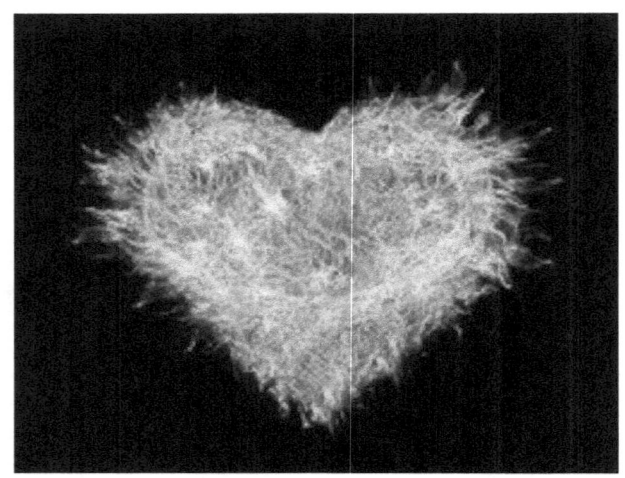

Your Darkness Is Shining

I. soil

in humble black gold
like downtrodden lifting all

seeds dreaming green
sleep like sparks

in the womb of the dark

II. sky

in longest night

when tulips aren't even on the tip
of a dream

cold creeps towards the center
of a hibernating heart

where a lowly sun is born
whispering secrets

III. silhouette

in the stretched pregnant hour
before the dance of the day

this hushed unrushed
unseen hanging chill

clings a damp cloak
skin tight on the fog face hymn of owl

while stars sing soliloquies

IV. soul

in your pitch-black sacred wound
that deep dull ancient ache

your darkness shines

a gorgeous throbbing face
—a lighthouse calling you to the shoreline
Of a ho homecoming

The Deeper We Crawl

The darker the eyes, the further we see,
slithering down in a slithery spree,
slithering up, slithering free.

In stillness, we flicker the world open
and feel all the vibrations

winding our bodies across the belly
of our earth

slithering out of our old
and into our new

powered by that old soul-song
of grandfather serpent
who knew the first rhythms.

The deeper we crawl, the brighter we burn.
slithering 'round with slithery turns
slithering in our slithery yearn

A Crack and Hidden Yes

Even the fabulously defeated
Coiled and feeling beaten
Wintered in and pinned with pain
Can't help but open up again

Have a crack and hidden yes
All's not black amidst the mess
Has a soft under the hard
And a heal for every scar

Protect the core...for sure, for sure
Bending inward so as not to bleed
But done with Love is done with life
And Light needs dark as dark needs Light

Its inner arms reaching out
Past the wound, past the doubt
And finds a way to come and play
The voice within as if to say:

We have a crack and hidden yes
All's not black amidst the mess
We will not coil hard and tight
We'll find the touch, and let the light

A Riff-Raff On Rifts and Rafts

Since the Great Descent has commenced
and the grand ol' ship is sliding so slick
into the Unlit Rift
to a cacophony of confusions

why not lend our glistening ribbits
to the bright and awful symphony of things?

why not keep our ears open
to freaky frogs and fungi friends
allying with the Otherwise?

why not build our rafts
with starfish imaginations
and chthonic confederacies

with mycelium magic and slug slime

fiddling a sweet tune into the vast
and fickle Field of Uncertainty?

Why not slip out of our rain boots
and tie dreamland suns to our dirty feet

turning on our heartache headlamps
and sun-lit grins as we remember
the Tender Pulse of things?

Why not place our fool-proof
amphibious wisdom and favorite fears
between the bookends of slave ships
and the campfires of the seventh generation?

Can you feel it?

We're becoming
(insert the deep drums here)
Beloved Ancestors—

So robust with courage
that we're inviting arrows
over for experimental dancing

to pierce the folds of our skin
where we are not yet looking

in order to feel the hidden artesian well of things
and the mad migrations
beckoning for emergence

including the syrupy ache of opening
ever-more fantastic cracks!

out of which our most fearless frogs
and moon-faced monsters crawl

with whom we eventually fall in love

getting us all giddy-up and go
to blast rainbow graffiti
on the walls of each other's hearts

and while some say that a party
for the dead and dying OverCulture
is not appropriate

it just might be time
for inappropriate celebrations.

We Dream the Butterfly

You only have to ask the butterfly
that a cocoon can be a safe haven

but also a guardian against the truth
that is arriving, if you linger in the threshold

Yet it is the abode of transformation—
if we're willing to surrender and disintegrate

Willing to trust that there's nothing
more practical than dying and resurrecting

which are the basic operating instructions
of the universe

willing to trust that ink black uncertainty
is necessary for shapeshifting

Willing to trust the ceremony
of our old bodies dissolving
becoming root-wings of the new

Yes, becoming goo is brutal

but holding onto old forms
is even more painful

We are imaginal buds
of what is trying to emerge

no longer having allegiance
to the caterpillar of us

but to dreams of liberation.

Pollinating wildflowers,
birthing wild new prairies—

We dream the butterfly.

(First published in *Trust the Ceremony, F*ck the Ceremony, Trust the Ceremony*)

Dear Mud

Dear mud,

This is a hard letter to write.

You know how there is a season
for everything? I feel
we were meant to be a season
for each other,
not a lifetime.

I do love you. You were such an important
part of the journey.

But I can't choose you. I'm sorry
our paths aren't aligned
any longer.

I'm writing this because I honor
our season together.

I so appreciate you
and what you bring to the world.

You are such a phenomenal force of nature!

You taught me so much,
about the trail of life
and about the trail of myself.

You showed me how to slow down.

To really be with things.

You showed me where I'd been.

To
be
careful
where
I
step.

But also how not to be afraid
of really getting in there
and getting dirty.

Oh I'll always remember the way
we mucked each other!

So slow and sensual,
so earthy and juicy,
so alive.

You showed me the texture
of my sacred shining wounds.

Where I was stuck, but also
how to let the words 'I'm stuck'
fall from my lips
and it be ok.

Yet you also showed
me how to get out.

It starts with saying the truth.

And doesn't everything come back
to that?

And the truth is
I can't do this anymore—
There's a path ahead
I need to explore
on my own.

So I have to say goodbye now.

I'm sorry. Please forgive me.
I forgive you for everything.

I know we did the best we could
with the boots and tools we had.

So I'm grabbing the ladder
of my own brave ribs
and with a gigantic sucking heave
pulling myself upward
towards the new sun.

I love you.
Goodbye.

So, Crack

Where you arrive at the end of one nation
and another begins, they tell you

but where an old self ends
and a new one opens up

you must discover yourself
over and over
through vast experiments of trial and t(error)

The kind of (t)error that has you thinking
you're floating untethered
away from the space vessel
and all form of things

Or are you one who thinks you know
good from bad
when all the things seem to break?

When foundation earth cracks
and space comes hurtling
through your bones?

Unravel more accurately
and sink into your silence
robust and cunning

but then embrace the kind of uncertainty
that has you planting dreams
for the seventh generation

the kind that adds a layer of fat
to your empathic system

Yes, Part of you wants to think
all the notes come up black

and part wants to keep chuckling
past the comet to make your own orbit

The part of you that,
like a meadow of wildflowers
wants into the world so bad
will do anything to make it happen

including leaping lupine
and flashing fuchsia
petaling upward umbeled and spiked

Or do you really think that meadow arrived gently
on wings of peace?

What of the ten million year preamble
of terrible upheaval
anticipating the beauty before you?

So, crack.

Break into the liminal space
with all the elegant pain you can muster

Forget all the fine tethers,
attractive and dead

Even fish have to jump out of their world
from time to time

Turn indigo and crack the crust
petaling your meadowed self
without restraint

until your chasmly scream
your unbound love
pure and unshackled
booms through all the worlds

Earth Will Soon Pour You Out

Persephone, are you not the author of your own notes?

Are you not indeed your own mother
living inside a seasoned gown?

The Underworld ties your hands down
in the unlit palaces

but what of your lungs and legs
and the crown upon your head?

Lather the golden leaves on your dusky skin.

Pour weeds from your eyes
and cry flowers.

Laugh dark and riotously to rival the rain.

I believe in you—it's going to be ok.

But you don't need me to lend belief—
Earth will soon pour you out.

Whose permission do you need but your own?

Do you not trust your own power?

You may forget for a bit,
but Spring will spill out of you
as easily as you now close your eyes.

All the old songs will be resurrected,
and the new will rise like a fresh breeze.

The Path Is Made

We're returning.

There is no path, pilgrim.

The path is made by crawling and clawing.

The path is made by climbing.

The path is made with caresses.

The path is made with compassion.

The path is made by contradictions.

Start crawling.

Mix the kernel of your truth—
that improbable spark
in the vastness—

with the clay of where you live,
deep with dreams.

It is your own dawn
looking Earth in the face
saying, "I remember you"

It is a longing long in seed form
worth a watering.

I Dispute This Passage No More

Out of the twelfth-month
midnightic pull, a murmur

sings itself vigorously
with all the force gravity
and the old unspeakable yearn
can muster

towards the rocks
and the source sea
a destiny pointed and unpent

How I with flow feel
both the heavy and light of love
robust and whole

I am really here
swallowing all unstoppable creeks

a mere bubble and not
a mere bubble

I hang my head low as the winter sun
and bold blending with cold waters
sweeping the sweet pang of fate
to which I am subscribed

Dipping ears wet I dispute
this passage no more

It hums me through the deep night
with the whisper

that all things in time
eventually find their flow

Flashes Buried Here

There are flashes buried here
in the hot sand of this life

Some are mirages
others are mirrors

some are red-hot miracles
awaiting the eye of your heart.

Who put them there
is not for us to know

it's not a place to dwell, but sometimes
you must cross the dry desert
to find your freedom sunrise

Even though it's been shining
through that ache within an ache
the whole time

If the rare hare has it
and the sagebrush is lush
and the moon shower
brings the cactus flower

you have absolutely no right
to just lie down
and bury your head in the sand

Keep gathering the impossible shimmerings—

Some are mirages
some are mirrors

and some are red-hot miracles
awaiting the eye of your heart...

That Poem Under Your Skin

That poem that lives under your skin?

That poem may be so far under your skin
you might need the raven's cry
to claw its way in at dawn

You might need an unkempt trickster
to fool your eyes

in order to fling a true word or two
from within your pretty vault

But then the poem will roll off your skin
all mist and moist
as an offering to the earth

It'll stain your fingers with beets
Your lips with wine
Your thighs with blood

It'll write your forehead with mud
Your back with her scratch
Your arm with Hafiz

Your story with a wound will shapeshift
and a wild coursing will resume

It'll entangle your head with the storm
Your hair with twigs
Your eyes with the moon

Or are you here to let your poem sleep
through it all?

Then form your raw rituals
and let the world nibble it awake

Serviceable Conduit

Don't feel bad for having forgotten—
Feel more.

Don't get out your impressive whip
just because you fell asleep yet again

The world already believes
all-too-brightly in mandatory punishment.

Instead, say Yes
to mandatory astonishments
of a world bent on beauty.

Conduct research into surrendering
to skin-on-skin contact with Mystery.

Inquire into being a serviceable conduit
for what wants to be created through you.

Practice over and over
an abundant alignment
that longs to enflesh some wondrous thing

Offering your Life
in ceremonial commitment
to the Grand Metabolism.

The Gift

The Gift is a delicious deformity,
not a recognizable shape

It is an absurd gesture,
not an obligatory posture

It shall not contort
for the comfortable gaze

It will not bend the knee
for daylight praise

Its sacred script is scrawled on dungeon walls
not legible to sun-soaked eyes

It may look clumsy,
waltzing with all the big and little deaths

It may sound like silence or a siren,
being intimate with well-traveled wind

or feel harsh to the touch
having followed great granitic ways

The taste is acquired,
having caught mulch and midnight in its beak

Committed to that deepest root,
it surrenders all easy prizes

Like all good dark allies,
it was born in the basement of things

its chthonic love holding the flame
in its luscious lap

Robust in its caress,
skilled with its talons

It risks the universe
to create the universe

The Gift is a delicious deformity,
not a recognizable shape.

The Experiment Isn't Over

What if we don't really know
if the universe is expanding
or contracting

or both?

because we don't know
how willing or able we are to stay open

We ask ourselves:

Can I withstand the crunch?

What if like a buried seed
the real question lurking is:

Can I bear the sound
of my shell cracking open

with that sweet amber pain
mistaken for trouble?

Our ears pick up the warbler's woo
suggesting dawn is here yet again

and we breathe a little deeper

Suggesting these cycles
are built into everything

Suggesting the experiment
isn't over

Rising Like a Blessing, Unbidden

They don't tell you the curious things
that can happen
the moment you arrive at a center

Like how the sounds of being alive
pour in and out of you
and there's no telling who is pouring whom

How even more ears open
as trust unfolds like a reckless dawn
rising like a blessing, unbidden

How even as the world drips itself awake
you already become nostalgic
for the journey

that even as you feel
into the tender sigh of stillness

the spiral is where we play
at becoming who we are

How an ancient joy is always there
chirping in the blood

layering itself exquisitely
alongside a precious pain
from seeing the sacred struggle

but that pain is not your enemy—
it is the magic and medicine

without which you cannot do

what you are meant to do

and even cobwebs are held gently
in that soft pillow of deep time

A pang of understanding emerges:
There's not much you can say

Not much you *should* say
as all shoulds fall away

silent as the moss that's been with you
the whole way

All that is needed is here
in the form of a bright breath—
Your face making the shape of peace
your feet flowing towards new worlds.

ABOUT THE AUTHOR

Ryan Van Lenning, M.A., is author of *Trust the Ceremony, F*ck the Ceremony, Trust the Ceremony, One Bright and Real Caress, From Inside These Wild Ones, An Ambitious Silence, Re-Membering: Poems of Earth and Soul,* and a collection of haiku, *High-Cooing Through the Seasons*. His new collections *Becoming Beautiful Barbarians, Then Yeses Come Bubbling,* and *Riverever* will be released throughout 2025-26. He is the 2019 recipient of Jodi Stutz Poetry Award by Toyon Literary Magazine and his poetry appears in various poetry journals and the book *A Walk with Nature: Poetic Encounters That Nourish the Soul* and *Behind the Mask: 40 Quarantine Poems from Humboldt County*.

Ryan is Founder of Wild Nature Heart, supporting people to re-connect with the wisdom of both inner and outer wild nature, to live their callings into the world, and to assist in the work of repairing broken belonging during this Great Turning. He is a teacher, ecotherapist and wilderness rite-of-passage guide and lives among the forests and rivers of Northern California. He facilitates 6-week workshops called Write Your Wild River, Earth Intimacies, and Deep Belonging a couple times a year.

ABOUT WILD NATURE HEART

Wild Nature Heart supports people to connect with the wisdom of inner and outer wild nature, to embody our wholeness, and to live our wild purpose into the world in order to inhabit our particular niche in the ecosystem of healing and justice. Through 1-on-1 ecotherapy, earth-rooted mentoring, custom and group wilderness rite-of-passage ceremonies, and various Deep Belonging courses, ecospiritual workshops, and seasonal gatherings, Wild Nature Heart cultivates an ecospirituality that nourishes our deep belonging in the animate web of life in order to do the decolonial work that we are called to do in this moment of the Great Turning.

Wild Nature Heart believes that to cross this threshold into species maturity with a next-season guest pass we must keep our imaginations robust and make moves that subvert inherited paradigms of fear and supremacy. We are being invited to fall through the inherited maps into new territories towards collective liberation. As crises continue to invite us across thresholds of initiation, we crack open the paved highways of our hearts and bodies to allow the tributaries of our holy longings and wild purpose to flow in and out.

The journey is both a daily and life-long practice, as much as it is multi-generational and multi-species. We practice simultaneously being both death doulas to the world that is dying and birth doulas to the one being born. *www.wildnatureheart.com*

TITLES IN THE *RE-MEMBERING* SERIES

The book that began it all:
Re-Membering: Poems of Earth and Soul

The 75 poems in *Re-Membering* are an unabashed celebration of the sensuality of wild nature. Redwoods reach without apology towards the sky, and rivers flow with unflagging energy towards the ocean. This collection re-members Ryan's personal explorations into wild nature, but it also re-collects for all of us a time when our kinship and inter-connectedness with the natural world was self-evident, and invites us to fully re-inhabit and say "Yes!" to our sensual natures, our animal bodies, our playfulness and creativity, connection, mystery, and our instinctive love for this beautiful, sentient Earth.

"Ryan's poetry speaks deeply and clearly to the awakening to our true interconnected nature, which is the only way we can transform our world."
—Molly Young Brown, author of Coming Back to Life: The Updated Guide to the Work That Reconnects (co-authored with Joanna Macy)

One Bright and Real Caress
Book 2 in the *Re-Membering* Series

*Build an altar at each moment
with a goodbye on the tip of the tongue.
Slow dance drunk in the robust now.
Strap the searchlight around your ribs and shuffle like a
crescent moon over all your little resistances.
Can we be here now? Really be here?*

These are some of the invitations lurking in the poems of *One Bright and Real Caress*. This collection is a celebration of the moment. Of not escaping. Of impermanence. Of death as life partner. With syllables of relentless affirmation, these poems bring an unconditional caress over all the textures of life and our multitudes within. As an invitation to presence and an honoring of the all-too-real struggle to not flee the moment, these poems welcome every conceivable crescent mood, slivered and slow, with no aim but to edge out more and more into the whole ceremony and celebration.

**From *From Inside These Wild Ones*
Book 3 in the *Re-Membering* Series**

Gorgeous Storm

This gorgeous storm
keeps getting stuck in my teeth

as if I could bite-size my way
to destiny

When all I want
is to have it come
racing out my lungs

Like a waterfall plunging
over my luscious tongue

flooding all the landscapes
of my crooked life.

to join the wrens and warblers
and beloved lusts
of a wounded world
washing away the old debris

Please, Storm, please,
knock down the weak branches
of my being

Prune me for the season
I am meant to live

EXCERPTS FROM THE AUTHOR'S OTHER BOOKS

An Ambitious Silence

What it calls for is an elegant unraveling—
more accurate
and stunning than ever before

sinking into an ambitious silence,
robust and cunning

Do something useful for a change—Listen
so deep and richly
the big ear wants to open through you, remembering
all.

Be unfashionable—tear the ears off the false notes.

Shake your feathers and invite the fox and raven

Until oak reaches into you
and the deep waters gather.

Mud and Moon are your Elders.
You won't get far without them.

Chant Old Man Owl and Sister Dawn unto you.
That ancient place within beckons.

Unfold it into your bones
and drum your skeletal fragments
until they dance.

Then, like a humble apprentice
pay the tuition for your truth

bartering for the next bold season
with the currency of your heart

letting an unreasonable love
claim you like a throne

and walk your blessed seduction home.

From *Trust the Ceremony, F*ck the Ceremony, Trust the Ceremony*

Door-To-Mystery-Knows-Where

There is a door to Mystery-knows-where
and you are being invited to step through

The new doorway through which you pass
is framed with grander questions

where you'll pick up pieces left
in your canyons long ago

and find on the side
fragments resting by the fire

drinking ale for an evening tale
of dreams wanting to find their flesh

Put them in your wide-brim hat
and home in on your succulent belonging

becoming an obsessionate one
like a convict who loves their fate

This is the door to Mystery-knows-where
and you are being invited through

From *Becoming Beautiful Barbarians*
(Forthcoming)

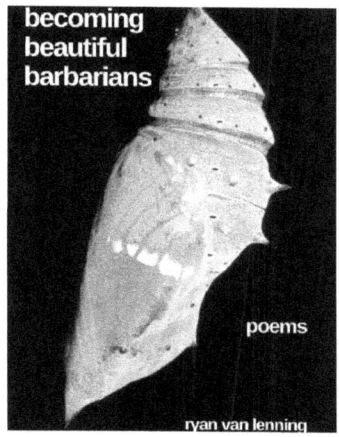

Off-Script

This is not a dress rehearsal.

This is an undress rehearsal—
We're undressing the stories
we've rehearsed for far too long.

This is not a blockbuster movie.

This is composter cinema—
The only heroes that will be rushing in
are the ones we see naked
in the morning mirror.

And that is more than enough.

With thistles and a raven's beak
we tear up the scripts we inherited.

They are what got us into the Big Trouble.

Liberation is leaking out
of every page of the book we are writing.

There is no script worth a damn
that doesn't include the voice of the river
the cries of our ancestors
or the longings living in our bones.

For each mouthful of empty-calorie modernity,
we create a meal
of new melodies.

For each megabyte of consumption,
we create a terabyte
of participatory dreaming.

With each breath we forge
strange and novel toys
in service to the Grand Metabolism.
We are preparing a buffet of the future.

www.ingramcontent.com/pod-product-compliance
Lightning Source LLC
Chambersburg PA
CBHW070638030426
42337CB00020B/4071